# Cinderella Claps Back

## The Reckoning

This book is a work of fiction. The names, characters and events in this book are the products of the author's imagination or are used fictitiously. Any similarity to real persons living or dead is coincidental and not intended by the author.

The content associated with this book is the sole work and responsibility of the author. Gatekeeper Press had no involvement in the generation of this content.

Cinderella Claps Back: The Reckoning
*First Edition*

Published by Gatekeeper Press
7853 Gunn Hwy., Suite 209
Tampa, FL 33626
www.GatekeeperPress.com

Copyright © 2024 by Traci Claywell
All rights reserved. Neither this book, nor any parts within it may be sold or reproduced in any form or by any electronic or mechanical means, including information storage and retrieval systems, without permission in writing from the author. The only exception is by a reviewer, who may quote short excerpts in a review.

Library of Congress Control Number: 2024944161
ISBN (hardcover): 9781662955082
ISBN (paperback): 9781662955075
eISBN: 9781662955068

This book is dedicated to my own godmother,
Leslie Quesenberry Simonet,
of Big Stone Gap, Virginia,
who watches down on me from heaven.

Who nourished my imagination and early
love of reading with a new book
every month of my childhood.

To this day my favorite possessions are the hundreds of
books throughout my home that stare back at me with
patience and encouragement, their authors pushing me to
stop being afraid and to believe in my voice.

Brava Leslie, and all the people who encourage children to
read, to dream, and to embrace their own possibilities.

And to the girls and boys of America,
including the ones yet to be born.
May your futures be filled with peace and freedom.
May your voices be heard.
May your choices be your own.

# *Cinderella Claps Back*

## The Reckoning

*A modern day fairy tale*
**By Traci Claywell**

gatekeeper press™
Tampa, Florida

When the late-night news of a secret plot to overthrow the government arrived at the Palace, where the late King Charming once reigned, a meeting of Queen Ella's Cabinet was called immediately. Nine of the realm's ten highest counselors scurried to the Round Table as the clock struck midnight, determined to sweep away this unprecedented threat.

"Good evening, everyone," said Queen Ella breathlessly as she burst through the door, greeting her advisors with a look of both concern and determination. "Thank you for showing up so unexpectedly at such a dreadful hour."

Each of her advisors pushed back their cushioned seats and stood ready, nodding back to her with the same solemn look. Everyone knew Queen Ella's aversion to the number 12, thus compounding their worries.

Ms. Snow White, Ella's Minister of Labor, who always sat to the Queen's right, helped her to her royal seat. Ms. White was known for her great ability to manage different types of personalities. Whether happy, grumpy, or even dopey, Snow

White knew how to make the full spectrum of characters work at anything, even things they didn't want to do. And they whistled, too. Unless they were sleepy.

Once Queen Ella was seated, Ms. White addressed the room.

"You may be seated," she said, and then looked to her left, eager to hear what the Queen had to say.

Ella took a few seconds to compose her thoughts, her eyes closed tight beneath her furrowed brow. She sent a quick private prayer to her fairy godmother and then looked around the room at this tight clique of characters who had proven through their own personal struggles that they knew how to conquer adversity.

For instance, Ella's most trusted advisor ~ after Ms. White ~ was Mrs. Shirley da Seneca, whose legendary reading habits had made her the most erudite person in the land. Seneca, as she was called, was the Minister of Justice and was most insightful, proving especially discerning in her handling of white ruffle crime.

Ella's Minister of Agriculture, Mr. Jack Bean, with his uncanny knowledge of agronomy and cloud patterns, had completely eradicated hunger in the realm, resulting in huge successes in education and innovation in the workplace. Because of Mr. Bean, poverty had been eliminated and the people were thriving. And even though he sometimes took unnecessary risks and could disappear for days, Queen Ella adored Jack and his acumen.

Ms. Gretel was another trusted advisor. Although the youngest of the group, she had a killer instinct, willing to fight, even destroy, anyone to protect those in her care. This is why she was the Minister of Homeland Security. In contrast, her twin brother, Hansel, worked with KINGDOMPOL as a chief hostage negotiator, using his clever verbal skills and quick thinking to save countless innocent children in less-fortunate places.

The Three Little Pigs served jointly as the Ministers of Housing and Urban Planning while Sirenita, with her extensive knowledge of both oceanography and special needs, served as the Minister of the Environment and Health and Character Services, respectively.

Closing out the small group was little Goldilocks herself as the Queen's official spokesperson, whose ability to explain sometimes controversial yet always complicated Palace decrees was always "just right."

The only character missing at the Table was the Queen's Minister of Treasure. A stingy, spiteful, ugly little man she had never truly trusted but needed, nonetheless, due to his mysterious ability to always find enough gold in the budget to pay the realm's expenses. His name was Rumpelstiltskin. And this time, he was the problem.

The Queen cleared her throat and began.

"I've called this emergency meeting tonight, this morning, whatever," she waved her hand at the clock, grimacing, "to make you all aware of an imminent plot to overthrow the Palace."

The faces of the Cabinet expressed shock and confusion.

"What do you mean, your Highness?" asked one of the pigs.

"Who would do such a thing?" asked another.

"I bet I know who would," muttered Jack Bean. "I never trusted that black-eyed pea one little bit."

"Who are you talking about, Jack?" asked Goldilocks.

"Look around," Jack answered. "Who's missing?"

Queen Ella nodded at her wise minister.

"Yes, indeed, Jack is correct. It has been revealed that Mr. Rumpelstiltskin, as witnessed by the Fairy Bureau of Investigation on Miss Charlotte's Dark Web, is plotting to lead an insurrection against the Palace and overtake our government."

"How?" signed Sirenita.

"Yes, and how do we know this?" followed Gretel.

Queen Ella turned to Ms. White.

"Snow, will you please?"

On cue, Snow White picked up the remote control and turned on a television mounted on the wall behind them. She pushed another button and the overhead lights dimmed. A few seconds later and the screen came to life showing a large smoky room filled with brown-coated wolves ~ those self-pitying outcasts in the kingdom, always sniffing, lurking, looking for trouble ~ standing shoulder to shoulder, the camera jostling as the mongrels jockeyed for position in the tight space. Slowly, the sounds and images became more clear. Lots of fur and lots of growls. Mugs of beer clunked amid shouts of excitement.

Soon, the camera zeroed-in on a simple stage completely bare. A flag hung on the wall beside it, a flag for a party. Not the Fairy Party, though, but a new party. An anti-Fairy party. It was called Fiery, the Golden Fiery Party. And its symbol was a flame of gold, huge and all-consuming, emblazoned on a background of blood-red cloth.

Suddenly, as if on cue, the crowd roared as Rumpelstiltskin himself took the stage, hobbling along on his two uneven legs, his twisted grin open and wide, revealing his rotten yellow teeth and oversized tongue. His rotund body was clothed in a suit that matched the flag, blood red, with stripes of gold, including a red and golden tie. His face was slightly orange, a bad attempt to cover the pock-marked divots in his pudgy face. His nose was enormous, as were his ears. But what stood out the most was his signature accessory, a big fat tuft of straw covering the top of his badly disguised bald head. Of all the hideous aspects to his physical self, his baldness was the thing that shamed him most. But, just like the straw that he could turn to gold, he assumed that it worked magic on his head, as well. It gave him comfort and he wore it like a crown.

Rumpelstiltskin looked out into the crowd and pumped his fists in the air in time as the wolves screamed his name.

"RUM! pel! STILTS! kin!

"RUM! pel! STILTS! kin!"

He gimped back and forth slowly from one end of the stage to the other, clapping back to the audience, his minions, his all-adoring tools. He knew they would believe anything he said. He was the only character who said things outwardly that they believed privately, but were too hesitant to say out loud. He removed the plugs from their private jugs of resentment, stirred their pots of bitterness, and electrified their disappointments into a blaze of self-deluded victimhood. In a nutshell, he validated their hate. And they adored him for it.

Rumpelstiltskin licked his slobbery lips as his eyes glazed with power. Seconds turned to minutes as the chanting continued. Rumpelstiltskin returned to the middle of the stage and, with his head held way back, eyes closed as if standing under a shower of golden rain, he raised both arms into the air in the form of a cross and soaked it up. The wolves howled even louder, eventually reducing his quadri-syllabic name to just one word.

"RUMP! RUMP! RUMP! RUMP!

They stomped their feet, pounding their torches and their pitchforks on the slick, wet wood below them. Glass could be heard shattering along the floorboards as many slammed their mugs to the ground, unable to contain the frenzy that boiled inside their barren souls.

Finally, Rumpelstiltskin brought his stubby little hands back down to his sides and looked out into the crowd. He put a crooked finger up to his lips, signaling them to shush.

Slowly, the volume decreased, until finally, when there was nothing to be heard but the heavy breaths of a few, Rumpelstiltskin spoke in a mock-whisper.

The throng leaned forward, straining to hear what their great leader had to say.

"My friends, my comrades, my fellow believers of the past..." He paused, watching them gaze at him with eager eyes and hungry hearts.

"Once upon a time, in this dear kingdom we call home, where our fathers and their fathers and all the fathers before them were born and lived and died, we thrived in a world where we were ruled by kings! By men! By those who, like us, understood that power resides in the physically gifted, the strong, the able. It is our birthright as men to expect to be led by men. Am I right?"

The wolves howled again, releasing the angst that had been festering in their hearts for three long years, ever since King Charming had died in a freak bow-and-arrow-in-the-face accident with a wealthy Palace patron.

"And YET!" Rumpelstiltskin stomped his foot and punched his palm for emphasis, spittle raining down on the first few rows in front of him.

"For the first time in our history, a woman, the Queen, has now taken the reins of the Palace. Never in our history has a king died without a prince, a son, to replace him. Until now. NOW! In our lifetime!"

Rumpelstiltskin's fury was loud and contagious. His orange face turned red as he paced back and forth, letting his words sink in.

"Queen Ella is now the sovereign of the land, reducing us from a Kingdom to a Queendom," he shouted, mocking the last word with contempt. "A throne she stole! From US! And what else? She has filled her Cabinet almost entirely with... women!"

The wolves howled angrily in their disgust.

"You should see them," Rumpelstiltskin continued, "with their princess crowns and long-flowing tresses, their dainty little hands and their soft, silken dresses!"

The crowd booed and shouted more insults.

"And their books, their little friends, and most of all, their good little moral codes. I tell you, every day that I sit at the Palace, pretending to care about the Queen and her little ideas, all I can think about is"—he paused for effect—"what I wouldn't do to put that smug little uppity HAG in her place, out of the Palace, and back to that dirty little fireplace with her ashy little hands and pathetic little chores.

What I wouldn't do to put her back into domestic servitude. Where she belongs! Where they all belong!"

Rumpelstiltskin raised his arms again into the shape of a cross and yelled one last line.

"We will not be replaced!"

The wolves went berserk, repeating the little man's words with violent energy. And then at some point, from somewhere in the back, one wolf changed the chant, and the words morphed from one howling cur to the next, spreading until the entire beer hall was shouting together.

"The queens will not replace us! The queens will not replace us! The queens will not re—

Click! Suddenly, the television turned off and the overhead lights came back on. The stunned Cabinet sat motionless, silently processing all that they had observed.

Snow White broke the silence. "I think we've seen and heard enough," she said.

"Is there anything else that you can tell us, Your Highness?" asked Seneca.

"The video continues for many minutes more with the same type of rhetoric and histrionics you just witnessed. However, towards the end, Mr. Rumpelstiltskin states that the attack on the Palace will take place in six days."

"And this video was shot...?" the third little pig queried.

"Two days ago," the Queen answered quietly.

"That gives us only four, no, three days to prepare!" Gretel yelped.

"This is true," agreed the Queen. "Now, I want all of you to go home and get as good a sleep as you can get under the circumstances. Tomorrow, we will begin our preparations for our defense." She paused before closing, solemnly, "May Fairy Godmother watch over and protect us all."

In unison, the Cabinet stood again as the Queen rose from her royal seat. Discreetly, she touched both Snow White and Seneca's hands on either side of herself and whispered, "Follow me to my upper chambers."

The threesome then walked through the doors that were held open by two liveried foxes and up the grand staircase to the Queen's private domain. The three plopped themselves into a soft spot of her choosing in front of a magnificent fireplace over which a portrait of King Charming hung, releasing deep sighs. Their common experiences of entrapment, envious relatives, cruelty and sadness, as well as the common experience of having to earn her own personal freedom through ingenuity and guile had created an impregnable bond between them.

"So," Ella began, asking the obvious. "What in this fairy-tale world are we going to do about, what did they call him...Rump?"

"I don't know, but whatever it is, we've got to act fast," answered Snow.

Silence ensued as the three sat in their own thoughts, brainstorming ways to eradicate the looming threat. Although the wolves of the land were a minority, they were prone to unpredictable violence and fed off of each other's aggression and rage.

For years the Charmings, first under the King and now Queen Ella, had tried to placate the wolves and provide them with roles that would give them pride and purpose.

But nothing less than all-out power would bring the wolves to a more peaceable mood. They wanted the world to operate under their rules, the rules that used to be, when they could blow down houses on a whim or gobble up little girls or even their grandmothers whenever they wanted. They wanted their world to return to a time when they were the top of the political food chain. But their rules were cruel and mean-spirited. And did not serve the general good. And so, they were overruled. Finally.

Until now, when Rumpelstiltskin was giving back to them the relevance they felt they had lost.

"Maybe we could call in a favor from the Pied Piper," Seneca suggested. "Since we dropped the kid-snatching charges once he returned all the children back to Hamelin, he owes us."

"What could the Piper do?" asked Ella.

"Oh, get Rump in a room with all the rats, maybe." Seneca grinned. "Make sure they're good and hungry."

Snow laughed. "That would be cannibalism, for sure."

Queen Ella sighed. "No, I'm afraid that wouldn't work. The last thing we need is another infestation of rats. The wolves are bad enough."

They kept thinking.

"What if we seized him up in Rapunzel's old tower?" suggested Snow. "Or turned him into a frog?"

"Interesting." Ella nodded, half-listening. "Now, how about this idea...who's thirsty?"

The two others nodded emphatically.

Ella tinkered with her bell. In a heartbeat, another liveried fox appeared, carrying a tray with each woman's drink of choice.

"Your Highness," he bowed, handing her a pumpkin-spiced latte. "Just as you like it."

Queen Ella took a sip.

"Oh, yes, perfect." She smiled gratefully.

He turned next to Snow White.

"Your appletini, Madam," he bowed.

"Ah yes, thank you, Mikko," she smiled. "As long as they're green and not red, I do love my apples."

Finally, he turned to Seneca with her crystal glass of chilled rosè wine.

"Madam," he bowed.

"Thank you," Seneca answered, her encyclopedic mind continuing to spin.

The butler left and Queen Ella lifted her drink into the air.

"To the Queendom," she toasted proudly.

"To the Queendom," Snow and Seneca echoed, lifting their drinks in tandem before bringing them to their lips. A sudden sharp ache brought Ella's attention to the floor. She lifted one foot, and then the other, studying them. Suddenly, with a deep frown, she clinked her drink on the table beside her in dramatic fashion.

"I don't know about you two," she said, standing up, "but I think it's time I invested in some new shoes. My feet are killing me."

Then, with dramatic emphasis, she faced the enormous fireplace and kicked one glass slipper, and then the other, off of each foot, sending them smashing against the hot bricks inside.

Seneca put down her wine glass and clapped loudly. "Brava! Finally! I've been waiting to see you do that for ages," she laughed.

"You don't know how much better that feels," Ella sighed. "Now, if we can just figure out how to let go of these corsets and brassieres and shapewear, we might be onto something."

"We could burn them," laughed Snow.

"You're right," Ella answered, not laughing. "After this fiasco is over, we'll do just that. I'll put out a decree next week."

The three continued to sip quietly, imagining a world without archaic body constraints.

"Speaking about feeling better, have you heard about Ambrosia?" Snow asked. "I hear she's out of rehab."

"Oh, is she now?" Queen Ella responded with compassion. "I know she's been struggling a long time with those pills. Her narcolepsy has been such a burden."

They were silent once again thinking of their friend and her struggles with her sleep disorder.

Seneca spoke next. "How are your stepmothers doing?" she asked.

The Queen coughed, nearly spitting out her coffee mid-sip.

26

"Goodness, Shirley, you might give me a little warning, couldn't you?" She laughed, picturing her evil stepmother in the little rubber room in which she now lived. Though it was an urban legend that the kind and gentle Ella had forgiven her stepmother and allowed her to live at the Castle with herself and the then-Prince Charming, the true story was that she didn't trust her at all and opted instead to send her to a sanitarium. Within a week, the doctors had diagnosed the stepmother as a narcissistic sociopath and a danger to society. And so there she had remained, ever after.

"She's doing fine," Ella answered, taking another long sip. "I find it interesting, though, that I get a letter from her every week, like clockwork, begging me to let her go free. Isn't it ironic?"

Snow nodded. "I get it. I mean, I get those types of letters, too. My stepmother, as you both know, is in the same hospital, but her diagnosis is different. Paranoid schizophrenia with delusions of grandeur. The doctors attribute it to her obsession with that mirror on the wall and all the things it said to her."

"I wonder what made them, the stepmothers, that is, so wicked," said Seneca. "Same thing with Hansel and Gretel's stepmother. In fact, all the stepmothers in this land seem to be overtly cruel. I've always wondered what made them so."

They sipped some more, each wondering why all the stepmothers ever created had turned out to be so evil. Such a mystery.

"So, where'd they put it?" Seneca continued. "The Magic Mirror, I mean."

"Actually, I had them lock it in storage high above us in the Palace attic," Ella answered. "I'd rather keep it safe here rather than allow it to fall into dangerous hands."

"But," Seneca retorted, "is it still dangerous?"

"Yes and no," the Queen said. "We had it analyzed by Gretel's team at Homeland Security, and they determined that the power of the mirror depends completely on the mental state of the character interacting with it, reflecting only ~ and exactly ~ what the viewer wants to see: the good, the bad, and the ugly."

"So, why have you kept it?" Seneca asked.

"I guess I've always considered it a secret weapon," admitted the Queen. "Something to have in my back locket...just in case."

"Just in case," Seneca repeated. "Just in case..."

Quietly, her fingernails began tapping on her wine glass.

Tap. Tap. Tap, tap, tap.

Snow looked at Ella and Ella looked at Snow.

Tap tap tap. Tap tap tap.

They both raised their eyebrows.

"I think we know what that sound means," Snow smiled.

"Yes, we do, Snow. A pot of gold or ~ dare I say ~ a Queendom for your thoughts, Shirley da Seneca," coaxed Ella with a wink.

Squinting into the dancing flames, Seneca continued her hypnotic tapping a few more times, and then blinked in quick succession. The tapping stopped and her focus returned to the here and now.

Queen Ella and Minister White leaned in, eager to hear what the Minister of Justice had to say.

"Ladies," she said, a twinkling smile splayed across her clever face, "I have an idea."

\* \* \* \* \* \* \* \* \* \* \*

It was two days later and Rumpelstiltskin was deep underground in the Woods outside of Charming Castle. For the last year, his band of wolves and other nefarious creatures ~ trolls and moles, jackals and giants, griffins and grendels, goats and goblins ~ all had been busy at work, digging and clawing an intricate web of tunnels. Inside they had mustered hundreds of weapons for their imminent invasion. Just weeks earlier, with the help of some warlock's dark invisibility magic, they had reached the underbelly of the Castle without anyone on the inside knowing. Tomorrow evening ~ at midnight, of course ~ Rump and his cult of hairy henchmen could finally put into action the plans they had been perfecting for over a year: infiltrating the Castle from below and spreading throughout like roaches, until every nook and cranny was taken. And then he, Rumplestiltskin, would ascend to the throne as King. King Rump. When things of the past would once again become the present. When men would rule, and women would acquiesce. When wrong would be right, and right would be wrong. The way things always had been before, and would become again. Forever and ever.

And Ella and her band of goody-two-shoes? They would be removed, banished forever, to the Towers. All of them. Except for Ella. For Queen Ella, Rump had envisioned something even more special. And it involved a wooden throne with glass constraints for her wrists and ankles, and rope, lots of straw, and of course, a mighty flame.

Rump was deep into these thoughts when a witch suddenly appeared above him on her broom, circling closer and closer, tighter and tighter, until finally landing with a loud *swoop*, bringing a rush of wind that reeked of an odd combination of rotten eggs, bad apples, and freedom fries. Now, this poor little witch, contrary to popular belief, was not wicked. In fact, she had the capacity to be a good little witch. Unfortunately, however, she had been told all her life that she was predestined, that she was supposed to be wicked, expected to follow the rules that her brethren had made, to follow in their footsteps and glorify their words and deeds.

Deep down, the witch wasn't truly wicked. She didn't really want to cause harm; she just wanted to belong. To be included within the circle of those with the power, to feel like she mattered, even if that meant silencing her own thoughts and ideas. Her need for acceptance, her fear of excommunication, trumped her conscience, and so she went along with Rump and the wolves and all the misguided brainwashing with which she had been indoctrinated her whole life.

The witch did not realize her own value, her own power. In some ways, she was afraid of it. Because if she actually owned her own power, she would be accountable. To not just the world, but to herself. And that was scary. It was easier to follow the dictates of others than to own her choices and decisions and mistakes. And so, the little witch chose to be wicked, to deny her own personal power, and instead became yet another instrument in Rump's box of dangerous tools.

"Mr. Rump, there is a message," she wheezed, handing him a roll of parchment sealed in wax and tied with a rose-red ribbon. The witch's knotted hands shook as she handed it to him, her warty face twisting in glee at finally being able to be so close to the future leader.

"It's King Rump to you," he sneered back, unable to bring himself to look at her hideous warts. "What is it?"

"I do not know, King," the witch answered, her voice shaking. "It was discovered overnight next to your spinning wheel at Rump Stump headquarters."

Since few of his associates ever read or composed anything of significance, it was rare for Rump to receive correspondence of any type.

"Let me see it," he demanded with a frown.

The witch placed the sealed parchment in Rump's stubby, outstretched hand, watching transfixed as he fondled it with ambivalent suspicion. He turned it over and over, studying it from all perspectives until his overwhelming curiosity won out. He ripped the seal in one jagged swipe and unrolled the page, bringing it close to his myopic eyes.

The witch watched with fascination as Rump read the note silently, saliva gathering at the corners of his sporadically moving mouth, his expression changing slowly from mistrust to surprise to, eventually, delight.

"What is it, my King?" the wicked witch asked with a pandering grin, her crooked fingers dancing together underneath her whiskered chin.

"Nothing!" Rump growled, lost in the message, having forgotten that he was in the presence of another. "Nothing at all!"

He wound the paper back into a tight roll and placed it forcefully inside the pocket of his jacket.

"Now, go away. And tell no one about this!" he ordered, refusing to look her in the face.

"Yes, my King," the witch agreed, head down and ashamed. She jumped back onto her broom and flew back to her perch in the trees, watching the wolves continue their preparations, all while Rump disappeared in another direction, skulking off through the Woods toward a certain beautiful princess's cottage, where he had been summoned.

* * * * * * * * * * *

BOOM! BOOM! BOOM!

The massive oak entrance to Ambrosia's little abode shook with a violent pounding.

"Come in," she sang out sweetly from her four-poster bed, lounging seductively upon lavender satin sheets, surrounded by plush pillows of various colors, shapes and textures.

Instantly, the door swung open, slamming into the wall behind it and causing several pictures and a vase filled with dark pink roses to crash to the ground. The humid evening air gushed through the gaping orifice, creating a storm of leaves and dust and other residue all around the candlelit room. It was a cacophony of chaos.

And in that doorway, that chaos, stood Rump in all of his hideous glory, feet spread wide, his tiny fingers gripping his crooked hips. He held his chin up high and took in the magnificent sight. Throughout the realm, it was no secret that the Minister of Finance had been enchanted with the this quintessential female for as long as anyone could remember. Maybe it was their mutual addiction to illicit pills, or maybe their common connection to spinning wheels. Who could know?

"I've been waiting a long time for this day to come," he pronounced, stepping into the room like the Boss he knew he was.

"Yes," Ambrosia answered just as directly. "As have I."

"Have you now?" he asked, wanting to believe her, but still suspicious. "Then, why now? What compels you to invite me to your chambers...now?"

Ambrosia looked down at her hands and the dainty handkerchief she was twisting with nervous energy.

"I've heard rumors that you will be King soon," she admitted, her shy eyes cast downward. "And I'd like to ask you to consider me for your..." She paused, slowly bringing her eyes back up to gaze deeply into Rump's.

"My...what?" he asked.

"Your qu—, I mean, your wife," Ambrosia admitted blushing, before adding, "and all that that entails."

Not convinced, Rump asked the next obvious question.

"And how did you come upon this ~ alleged ~ information?" he pressed.

"Oh, from my magic listening cap, of course," she answered, picking the famous red headdress off of the pillow next to her and holding it up as proof.

"And you've told no one else about what you have heard?" he continued, beginning to believe her. "Not Gretel, not Seneca?"

Ambrosia shook her head.

He studied her face for any hint of fakery, and then sneered, "Not the *Queen*?"

"Oh no, my darling, not a peep," she shook her head convincingly. "Why would I tell anyone of your plans if I could sit and stand and lie by your side every day and every night? Don't you believe me?" she asked, inviting him to her bedside with an outstretched arm. "My King, think of the possibilities."

And that was enough for Rump, who always came to conclusions quickly in situations such as these. Immediately, his head began to fill with all the lewd, necrophiliac thoughts he had imagined over the years with this enchanting nymph. Her porcelain skin, her buxom bosom, her innate comatose nature. As he stepped towards her, his lustful thoughts swirling like a flushing toilet, he suddenly felt the blood plunge from his head, forcing him to grab the nearest bed post for balance.

"Oh, my darling, you must be dehydrated," Ambrosia sympathized. "There, on the shelf." She pointed. "Get yourself a drink of water or maybe even your favorite, a shot of Goldshlager."

Agreeing that he did, indeed, need a drink, Rump hobbled to a nearby table and, ignoring the water, poured himself a shot of the golden elixir and then another, his mind racing. Tomorrow, the day of the insurrection, could not come soon enough!

After a third shot, Rump slammed his glass down and only then noticed the mirror, framed in thick bars of gold, hanging on the wall before him. He stared at it, mesmerized. Could it be? He had never seen himself look so, dare he say it, handsome. He stood tall and broad, his arms huge and muscular, his six-pack abs chiseled below his taut skin, not an ounce of fat in sight. His skin was smooth; his teeth, straight and white. And his hands? They were enormous.

"What is this?" he asked, unable to look away. "Is this the famous Magic Mirror?"

"Why, yes, it is," Ambrosia answered, leaving the bed and slinking her way up behind him, looking delicious in her baby blue gossamer nightie. In the reflection, Rump could see how he towered over her, the very first time he'd ever been able to look down on a woman instead of looking up. Aurora wrapped both of her hands around his right bicep and let out a soft sigh as she squeezed it with restrained longing. She pressed her body oh so gently into his. In the mirror, their eyes met. Although she was a sight to behold, his gaze returned to what truly turned him on.

Himself.

"Do I really look like this?" he asked, incredulously.

"Yes, my darling, you do!" She smiled, kissing his back softly. "Go ahead, ask it anything."

Rump basked in the stunning vision before him for a few seconds, and then cleared his throat. Timidly, he spoke.

"Mirror, mirror on the wall, who's the smartest of them all?"

A second passed, and then the mirror, in a deep, masculine voice, answered, "You are, my King."

Rump nodded, locking eyes with Ambrosia once more. She gave him another smile, another kiss on his shoulder.

"Go on," she whispered, emboldening him further.

Another question popped into his mind.

"Mirror, mirror on the wall, who's the richest of them all?"

In the same deep voice, the mirror spoke again, "You are, my King."

Gaining confidence, Rump asked a third question, the real question, the one that burned in his mind day and night.

"Mirror, mirror on the wall, who's the strongest of them all?"

Another pause, another second. And then another. The mirror was silent. Rump waited. Maybe it had not understood him.

"Mirror, mirror on the wall, who's the most potent one of all?" he repeated.

Again, silence.

Rump's forehead furrowed, confused.

"Don't frown," Ambrosia teased him with a smile. "Someone must have tampered with it." Then, she grasped his hands with both of hers and began pulling him away from the mirror.

"Come," she beckoned to his reflection with twinkling eyes. "I have something to show you."

"No, I need to know," Rump whined, turning his head back to the mirror. Ambrosia kept walking backward with Rump in tow as he kept yelling over his shoulder at the mirror, his petulant confusion mounting, until they finally reached the doorway through which he had entered, once upon a time.

"No, I'm not leaving until I get my answers," Rump shouted, pushing Aurora's hands away from him and turning back to face the mirror.

40

"Who's the strongest? Who's the most powerful?" he bellowed again. Over and over, he repeated his question, and over and over again, the mirror remained silent until, feeling exhausted, Rump finally gave up.

Ambrosia smiled.

"Minister Rumpelstiltskin, do you really want to know who is truly the strongest, the most powerful in all the land?"

Ambrosia's voice now sounded cold and unapproachable. No, worse than that, she sounded perceptive and smart. And cunning. Things were going downhill fast.

Rump turned to look at her, his eyes burning with questions. A cold feeling began to rain down on him, sending shivers down his crooked back. An idea, a hideous realization that he had been duped, sent alarm bells throughout his body. It was terrible enough that he may not, indeed, be the most powerful in the land, but even worse, if not he, then who? Who had the power?

"Do you?" Ambrosia pressed again.

Rump's hand flew to his mouth as the contents of his stomach threatened to burst out onto the floor.

NO, he did not want to know! Rump shook his head violently, unable to speak.

Suddenly, another voice, the most despicable sound of the realm, broke through the silence

"Let me tell you who has the most power, Mr. Rump."

Queen Ella stepped out from the shadows and into the candlelight, right up to Rump himself. She snatched the straw off of his head, returning what had appeared to be a beautiful shock of blonde locks to the shiny white dome it had always been. He screamed and reached up to cover his head in shame. He whipped his head back toward the mirror and realized with terror that his old reflection was back. He was still the grotesque ogre he had always been. He turned to Ella in a rage.

"You nasty woman!"

Suddenly, something amazing began to happen. Sparks of light began to shoot out from the mirror in all directions. It began to quiver and shiver, to shake and quake. Soon, the ground beneath them convulsed with latent energy, growing more and more intense, until finally, the mirror shattered into millions, (not billions), of pieces.

Rump ran screaming from the cottage to the nearest rock and crouched down, covering his head with his arms, where he sat cowering in fear. Hearing footsteps approaching, he closed his eyes tighter, ready for whatever was about to pounce on him.

But it was only Ambrosia. She touched him gently, saying, "Rump. Rump, open your eyes, it's okay. It's over."

"What do you mean?" he asked, opening one eye to look, just in case.

Still feeling queasy, he knew something wasn't right. There was too much light, too much sunshine. He began to hear voices behind him in the distance. Female voices. The vilest sound in the world. Women talking.

"Turn around," Queen Ella commanded. "I think it's about time you learned who truly has the power you so desperately crave."

Realizing he had no choice, Rump slowly turned to face the sounds at his back. And what he saw shocked him. What had once been a huge, wide-open meadow was now filled with hundreds, thousands, untold numbers of faces staring back at him. Female faces. Old and young, tall and short, thin and thick, beautiful and disgusting, and everything in-between. There were princesses and housemaids, mermaids and match girls, witches and Gypsies and fairies and godmothers.

But it was not just women. Out in the thick crowd of characters, Rump noticed some wolves in the mix. Here and there, they had joined with the females.

Rump looked with horror as the faces stared back at him, eyes filled with disdain. Their disgust, along with their rage, was palpable. He realized that, unlike the mirror that had just lied to him, these characters ~ these women, and some men ~ were the real reflection of his true self. The Emperor, indeed, along with no hair and no money, had no clothes. And without his 'roid-raging misogynistic thugs licking his boots and egging him on, he also had no power. He was impotent, after all. Rump's legs buckled, and he fell to his knees, weak and alone.

"Why are there wolves out there, and witches, too?" he whined. "Why won't they save me? Don't they love me?"

"I don't know, Mr. Rump. Do they?"

Like a wave, beginning at the front and slowly moving backwards the sea of faces stepped away from each other, creating an open path that reached deep into the crowd. And from that path emerged another character, looking young and small and vulnerable, a girl whose entrapment by wolves had made an everlasting impression on her psyche. Both she and her grandmother had suffered greatly at the hands ~ and the mouths, and other unmentionable parts ~ of wolves. And since then, she was determined to never let herself, or any other girl, be caught up in any of their terrifying tricks again.

It was Little Red Riding Hood, and she stepped out from the shadows and marched up to the little man with a Grimm look of determination.

"Do the wolves still love you?" She repeated his question to him. "Probably. Maybe..."

"Then why are they standing with all of"—he flicked his arm out toward the still-growing crowd—"them?"

"Because, maybe, just maybe," she reflected, "more than they love you..."

Little Red looked back out to the crowd, searching out the mothers and the fathers with laser focus.

"Maybe, they love their daughters more," she answered.

Rump's jaw dropped like a bomb. A thought like that had never, ever crossed his mind.

"And their daughters," followed Ambrosia.

"And their daughters," added Ella. "And yes, of course, their sons, too."

Thinking of Goldilocks, Ella looked out into the crowd, her subjects, who looked to her for guidance and decided to address them directly. She stepped onto Ambrosia's veranda and placed herself in a prominent position, with Snow White and Seneca following, taking their normal places beside her. Standing together, the three presented a triple threat of vision, intelligence, and grit, stirring the people's hearts with confidence, and hope. The Queen began.

"*All* children, *all* people, suffer when wolves are in power," Ella proclaimed. "They devour the power of everyone else for their own selfish delights and crude impulses!"

Nods and muttering of agreement rippled through the audience. Ella continued.

"We must have a realm that operates on fairness and justice and peace! No more 'might makes right.' It is our country! It is our choice!"

Her words struck a chord, and the crowd began chanting them, growing increasingly louder with each iteration.

"Our country, our choice! Our country, our choice!"

After a spell, Queen Ella motioned for the crowd to listen once more, and they did.

"Now, it is time for you, the individual characters who crave freedom and justice, who long for equity and peace, to go out to your own villages and do everything in your power to make sure the wolves in the realm never have the opportunity to rip those ideals away from the rest of us ever again!"

The crowd cheered, eager to return home to fight for the world they wanted, where books were never burned, and ideas flowed like water. Where power was transferred peacefully, and the law was never confused with violence. Where the minority had the same rights as the majority, and religion took comfort in one's heart, not plastered on public walls. Where every character had a say, and a right, to their personal beliefs and decisions, and those who aimed to interfere with those rights were held accountable.

"And you," Queen Ella said, turning to look at the pathetic Rump crouched at her feet, "You, dear sir, have no rightful place here anymore."

"Please, don't hurt me," he whimpered. "I promise I'll be good from now on."

The Queen just stared at him, shaking her head.

Rump trembled. "Are you going to lock me up?"

Ella turned to the strong, brave girl before her, who along with Gretel and Goldilocks and Jack, she secretly believed to be best-suited to lead the realm in the future. The next generation: wise and aware, conscientious and committed.

"Red, give the signal."

As directed, Little Red Riding Hood reached into her satchel and whipped out a flare. She aimed it into the sky, and fired. Suddenly, a wave of pink smoke blew across the sky, so huge and strong and all-consuming that there was no denying its power. And, on cue, the crowd began to close in around Rump, whose shrill voice could be heard throughout the Woods, squealing like a little pig as the throng gathered him up and deposited him in a secret location...

...And it was there, until the end of his days, where he was forced to sit in front of a television, every day and every night, and watch as all the good women and all the good men kept winning, and winning, and winning.

Rumpelstiltskin was never heard from again, leaving the big bad wolves with no choice but to return to their pathetic little chores in their pathetic little lairs and dream of the days of old. Days that would never come again.

And led by Queen Ella and her wise and able Cabinet, the Queendom ~ including all the mothers ~ the godly and the step and everyone in-between ~ and all the little girls, and all little boys, and all who lived by good moral codes, they all lived peacefully ~ and freely ~ ever after.

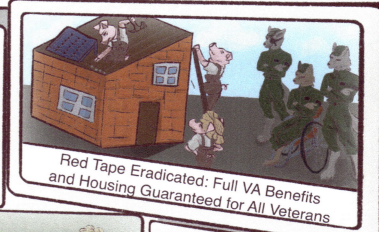

# Thank you

The book you are holding in your hands right now, *Cinderella Claps Back: The Reckoning*, would never have been born without the guidance and help from many people, near and far.

I must begin with my precious husband and son. Thank you for believing in me and taking up the tasks at home while I was consumed with publishing my first book! I had so much to learn, so many rookie mistakes! But you never complained. Your faith in me kept me going through the hard times. Believe me, no matter where I was, you were always on my mind. I love you both so much!

To Gloria, thank you for being the nurturing mother to my boy when I was not able to be. Thank you for your feedback about the story, the illustrations, and your overall encouragement. We would not be the same family without you.

To my (now) friends in Ukraine, Olena T. and Vlad, who managed the team of illustrators who created the beautiful scenes in my story. Olena, in three short months, you worked so hard and so late almost every night, making sure that my project came to life as promised. The hundreds of emails we sent back and forth over seven time zones are a testament to your dedication. From now on, in my mind, the letters O and T will stand for "Over Time." Thank you from the bottom of my heart!

And Vlad, thank you for making me laugh during our creative ZOOM calls. Even during blackouts from Russian drones and having to work through the sounds of bombs exploding near and far, you kept the focus on my story and my progress. I'll never forget you! Now, in the rhythm of the Village People's "YMCA", let's sing!

"I-C-B-M! I-C-B-M-m…"

To Susan and Jonathan, thank you for your constant concern, advice, and encouragement, always answering my calls for help when I struggled. You are my friends for life!

To three special Claywell cousins:

Leigh Anne, for decades now, you have supported me and my family when we needed it most in any way you could. Thank you for loving me and always being an honest voice with a kind heart.

Debbie, thank you for your honesty and telling me that my ending was not satisfying enough. I spent more time on it and beefed it up considerably. Looking back, I know your advice was the difference between Meh, and alright! Authors need honest feedback and yours came in the nick of time.

Jennifer, thank you so much for your enthusiasm for this story and others. Thank you for talking me through my anxiety and offering fantastic practical advice on the techie side of things. I love you all!

To Jacqui, Marie, Andrea, and Lauren, thank you for the professionalism you brought to the business side of my book. I will try to live up to the image you have created. :)

To my team at Gatekeeper Press: Rob, Trinity, Jessica, Lauren, and Luis, Thank you for bringing this book to fruition and living up to what you promised back on May 30, 2024. I know that bringing an 8.5"x11" full color illustrated book to market in less than four months was miraculous, but you and our Ukrainian artists made it happen. Thank you for putting up with my perfectionism. You run a tight ship and I am so grateful that I chose you!

To my family, Mom, Daddy, Christopher, Brett and Tamara: I send enormous gratitude to each of you for supporting me and loving me in your own individual ways. Although we disagree about many things, one thing that is undeniable is our loyalty to our family and to one another. I love you with all of my heart. Thank you for sharing this journey with me.

And to Brett specifically, thank you for believing in me and having my back for decades, all the way back to Beaufort. Thank you for the time and energy you could not afford to dedicate to me and my project, but did anyway. I believe in you, too.

To the rest of my family and friends, near and far, too many to name here, who have supported and cheered me on through the many years I've been writing about writing, I thank you. Thank you for taking the time to actually read my work and respond with feedback. You know, and I know, who you are. And I **really** appreciate you.

And last, but certainly not least...

To the women who came before us, who stood up against injustice and inequality, in whatever ways they could, both publicly and privately, who demanded that their rights, their work, and their talents be recognized, and who did not quit until their minds, their bodies, and their status were "created equal."

I thank you.

To all the women who came before us, thank you for speaking, writing, marching, and sometimes languishing in jail so that today we can casually walk up to a ballot box and vote...

...so that we can attend school and attain any degree of which we are capable, and by extension, enter into nearly any profession...

...so that we can participate in athletics, and be funded the same as the boys...

...so that we can have private bank accounts, credit, and loans without asking permission from our husbands...

...so that we can access contraception and determine on our own if we want to have a child, and if so, when...

...so that we can pursue happiness just as as our founding parents imagined, liberated and unencumbered.

Thank you!

Traci Claywell